science@work
Machines

ENGINES, ELEVATORS, AND X RAYS

By Janice Parker

RSVP

RAINTREE
STECK-VAUGHN
PUBLISHERS
A Steck-Vaughn Company

Austin, Texas

www.steck-vaughn.com

Published by Raintree Steck-Vaughn, an imprint of Steck-Vaughn Company

Library of Congress Cataloging-in-Publication Data

Parker, Janice.
    Engines, elevators, and x rays: the science of machines /
  by Janice Parker.
      p.   cm. — (Science [at] work)
    In ser. statement "[at]" appears as the at symbol.
    Includes bibliographical references.
    Summary: Discusses different kinds of machines, from digital thermometers and jet engines to elevators and microwave ovens, describing how they work and how they are used.
    ISBN 0-7398-0142-2
    1. Engines—Juvenile literature. 2. Elevators—Juvenile literature.
3. X rays—Juvenile literature. [1. Machinery.] I. Title.
TJ147.P35   2000
621.43 21—dc21   99-041594
                                        CIP

Printed and bound in Canada
1 2 3 4 5 6 7 8 9 0   04 03 02 01 00

Project Coordinator
Rennay Craats
Content Validator
Lois Edwards
Design
Warren Clark
Copy Editors
Ann Sullivan
Margaret Cook
Kathy DeVico
Layout and Illustration
Chantelle Sales

Photograph Credits
Every reasonable effort has been made to trace ownership and to obtain permission to reprint copyright material. The publishers would be pleased to have any errors or omissions brought to their attention so that they may be corrected in subsequent printings.

Air Canada: pages 5 bottom right, 31; **Alberta Technology, Research and Telecommunications:** page 14 left; **Carmie Auger:** page 4 bottom; **Ballard Power Systems Inc.:** pages 28, 32 bottom, 35; **Calgary Police Service:** page 22 bottom; **Corel Corporation:** pages 3 center, 19 top, 26 left, 27 bottom, 30 bottom, 42 top right, 43 top left; **Rob Curle:** pages 4 top, 10, 11 top, 13 top, 24 right, 37; **Eyewire Incorporated:** background pages 2–3 and 44–48, pages 5 top right, 6 top, 14 top, 17 both, 32 bottom, 35, 41; **John Fowler:** cover right; **General Motors:** cover background, pages 3 bottom, 23 top, 25, 27 top; **Intel Corporation:** page 24 left; **C. McGinnis:** page 26 top; **Sorcha McGinnis:** pages 7 left, 19 bottom; **Michael McPhee:** page 4 middle left, 6 left, 8, 15 right; **NASA:** page 5 bottom left, 23 bottom; **National Aviation Museum, Ottawa, Canada:** page 30 top; **Nobel Foundation:** page 33 bottom; **Photodisc, Inc.:** pages 3 top, 5 top left, 9 top, 12 top, 16 top, 21 bottom, 32 top, 33 top, 34, 39, 43 top right, cover left; **Picker International Inc.:** page 36; **Skylon Tower, Niagara Falls, Canada:** page 18; **Visuals Unlimited:** pages 16 bottom, 38, 40; **Wright University:** page 29.

Contents

Have you ever

checked the time on a clock,

used a remote control on your television,

or flown in an airplane?

If so, you have used some of the many machines that have been developed by scientists, engineers, and inventors. Machines are devices that help people do things better, faster, or more easily. We use hundreds of different types of machines every day. Machines can be very simple, such as the wheel. They can also be complex, such as an airplane, which is made up of many machines working together.

Without science, there would be no machines. All machines are made by people. We are constantly inventing new machines that affect our lives. Machines can perform tasks faster than people can. They often allow us to do more and have more free time in a day. Although machines are designed to help people, they can sometimes cause trouble. Engineers try to create machines that make our lives easier without harming other people or the Earth.

FINDING LINKS

Society

Most people could not imagine living without machines. They help keep us healthy and safe and make our lives easier at home and at work. Despite this, machines do not always affect us in positive ways. Some people believe that machines, especially computers, replace jobs in the workplace.

The Environment

Many machines, especially those powered by electricity or fuel, can add to pollution of the environment. Most automobiles, for example, are powered by gasoline or diesel engines. Engineers are trying to create new machines that pollute less. Non-polluting vehicles are now being developed.

Technology

Machines are the product of technology. We rely on many machines, such as cars, computers, and refrigerators, in our everyday life. New technologies in medicine, such as **CAT scanners**, help to save lives.

Careers

Almost every career involves the use of some kind of machine. Airline pilots work with a very large machine—the airplane. X-ray technicians use an X-ray machine to help **diagnose**, or determine, the cause of medical problems. Bank tellers use a computer to keep track of people's accounts.

Machines at Home

"It's time for another load of laundry."

ry to count all of the machines that you and your family use in your home throughout the week. We rely on all types of machines to make our home life easier and more enjoyable. Our homes contain machines to wash and dry clothes, machines to keep and cook food, machines for communication, and machines for entertainment.

Many of the machines in our homes were invented within the past one hundred years. Most of us use them every day without knowing how they work. We usually only think about these machines when they stop working and need to be repaired. Today we could not imagine living without all of the helpful machines in our homes.

How do microwave ovens work?

Gas and electric ovens cook food with heat. The heat cooks the outside of the food first, and then moves inward. Microwave ovens are much smaller, and they cook food more quickly than other ovens.

Microwave ovens use **radiation**, high-energy particles or rays, to cook food. Microwaves are electromagnetic waves, which are electrical and magnetic vibrations that travel through the air. Microwaves enter food and heat it evenly. As the microwave rays move through the food, they hit water, as well as sugar, fat, and salt molecules, and make them flip back and forth rapidly. The flip-flopping molecules rub against other molecules in the food. This rubbing together, called **friction**, heats the food.

Radiation can be dangerous to human health. Microwave ovens have thick walls to prevent radiation from escaping the oven. Microwave ovens use much less electricity to heat food than other ovens. Because of this, they are less harmful to the environment.

BYTE-SIZED FACT

Microwave ovens were invented by physicist Percy Le Baron Spence in 1946. He discovered that microwaves could be used to cook food after high-**frequency** radio waves melted a bar of chocolate in his pocket.

How a Microwave Cooks Food

1. Microwaves "bounce" off the inside walls of a microwave oven and penetrate the outer surface of the food (in this example, a potato).

2. The microwaves cause water molecules inside the potato to move and bounce off each other, causing friction.

3. The friction produces heat. This heat spreads into the center of the potato to cook it.

How do refrigerators keep food cold?

Refrigerators keep food at a constant cool temperature. Without refrigerators, we would not be able to keep food fresh for several days at a time. Refrigerators prevent food from becoming dangerous to eat by slowing the growth of **microbes**, or disease-causing bacteria.

To keep cool, refrigerators use a chemical called a coolant. The coolant moves in a cycle through small pipes contained within the walls of the refrigerator. As the coolant moves through the pipes, it changes from a liquid to a gas and back to a liquid again. When a liquid **vaporizes**, or changes into a gas, it absorbs heat from its surroundings. This cools off the air and nearby objects. The coolant near the inside of the refrigerator vaporizes, cooling down the air and food inside.

As the coolant continues through its cycle, it begins to heat up again. When a gas turns into a liquid, it heats up the surrounding area. This is why coolant in pipes near the outside walls of the refrigerator feel hot.

The coolant takes heat out of food in a refrigerator. That heat is released into the room by coolant pipes at the back or bottom of the refrigerator.

VCRs and Television Programs

Videocassette recorders, or VCRs, are machines that make copies of television programs so that they can be played at a later time.

VCRs turn the sound and picture images from a television program into magnetic signals. These signals are recorded, or copied, onto a roll of magnetic tape. When the videotape is played back, the VCR changes the magnetic signals into electric signals. The television set converts the electrical signals back into picture and sound.

A VCR has two, four, or six video heads. The heads are inside the machine, attached to a round drum that spins. As the drum spins, the heads record the images onto the magnetic tape. The sound from the television program is recorded at the same time by an audio recording head. If there is already a television program on the tape, it is removed by an erasing head before it reaches the video heads. There is also an audio erasing head to erase the sound from previously recorded programs.

BYTE-SIZED FACT

The first videocassette recorder was made in 1956. The machine used two large reels. It was too large to use in homes, but it allowed television broadcasters to show taped programs for the first time. A smaller, inexpensive VCR was invented for use at home in 1969.

Families can use a VCR to record a television program while they are at work or school. They can watch it together later when everyone is home.

How do washing machines get clothes clean?

Before automatic washing machines were invented, clothes had to be washed and wrung out by hand. Automatic clothes washers are essentially sinks and washtubs attached to a motor. Washing machines contain a large washtub. A smaller washtub filled with holes sits inside the larger tub.

Washing machines are designed to follow certain wash and rinse cycles. Different types of clothes are washed on different cycles. Each cycle takes a different length of time and may use hot or cold water. Delicate clothes, for example, are run on a very short cycle with cold water so the clothing will not be damaged.

Clothes and laundry detergent or soap are put into the inside tub of the machine. Once the cycle is set, the tub fills with soapy water. When the tub is full, a post in the center, called the agitator, begins to move back and forth. This back-and-forth motion loosens dirt from clothes. When the wash cycle is finished, the

Many homes have an automatic washing machine and clothes dryer side-by-side to make it easy to do the laundry.

dirt and soapy water are drained away from the machine. The inner tub spins quickly to pull away as much dirty water as possible from the clothes.

The machine then begins its rinse cycle. The rinse cycle is similar to the wash cycle, but no soap is used. The tub fills again with clean water, and the agitator moves back and forth to loosen any bits of leftover soap or dirt. After rinsing the clothes and draining, the tub spins very quickly. This removes excess water from the clothes so they dry quickly.

How do pendulum clocks keep track of time?

For thousands of years, people had no accurate way to keep track of time. Early machines used to tell time, such as sundials and hourglasses, were useful but not exact.

The pendulum clock keeps very precise time. A pendulum is a weight at the end of a long rope or rod. The scientist Galileo Galilei found out how a pendulum could be used to tell time. He discovered that a swinging pendulum always takes the same amount of time to swing back and forth. This is true no matter how far the pendulum swings. Galileo also discovered that the length of the pendulum determined how much time each swing would take.

Grandfather clocks use pendulums to keep track of time. The hour and minute hands are each moved forward by separate gear wheels. As the pendulum moves back and forth, it turns an escape wheel. The escape wheel then turns the main gear wheel. The gear wheel moves the hands on the clock forward at a steady pace.

Pendulum clocks often make a steady tick-tock sound as the pendulum swings back and forth.

BYTE-SIZED FACT

Pendulums cannot be used to keep time on wristwatches. Older watches contained a tiny hairspring, a fine spiral spring, that wound up and unwound at an even rate. Most modern wristwatches use batteries to provide the energy required to move the hands.

Here is your challenge:

Tie an eraser to one end of a length of string to make a pendulum. Tape the other end of the string to the edge of a desk or tabletop. Start the pendulum swinging back and forth, and count the number of swings in 15 seconds. Shorten the length of the string, and count the number of swings again. What happens?

How do cameras work?

When you take a picture with a camera, the camera records the image as a photograph. Light rays enter a camera through its lens. The reflected light from an object hits the film inside the camera. Before a picture is taken, a camera must focus on the subject. To focus, the photographer adjusts the camera lens until the image appears clear. Some cameras must be focused by hand, while others automatically adjust the focus.

Next, the exposure must be chosen. The exposure is how much time passes when the photo is being taken. The exposure time depends on how much light enters the camera and the speed of the film being used. This is usually a fraction of a second. Many cameras focus and set the exposure time automatically.

Cameras record the light that reflects off all objects in its view. The light causes a chemical change in the film, capturing the image. Later, the film is **developed**. Developing creates a negative image. This means that the image is opposite—dark areas are light and light areas are dark. The film negatives are turned into photographs, or prints, when they are exposed to photographic paper.

Automatic cameras are very easy to use. The photographer can just "point and click" to take a picture.

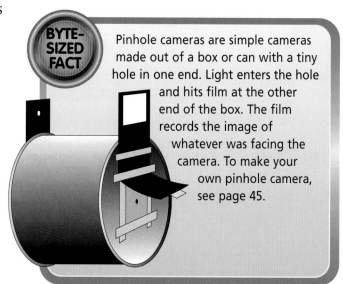

BYTE-SIZED FACT

Pinhole cameras are simple cameras made out of a box or can with a tiny hole in one end. Light enters the hole and hits film at the other end of the box. The film records the image of whatever was facing the camera. To make your own pinhole camera, see page 45.

Secure Buildings

Many special machines help keep our homes and other buildings safe. Some of these machines are simple devices, such as door locks, while others are quite complex. Many homes and office buildings have security systems to help protect the people and objects inside.

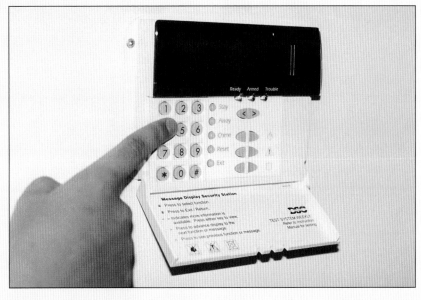

Security systems use electronic **sensors**, devices that react to light and heat, for example, to gather information about a building. If someone tries to break into a building, sensors detect the movement and send a message to the alarm system. The alarm system alerts the police or a security company.

There are several types of sensors used for security systems. Vibration sensors are placed on windows. These sensors detect any movement of the glass. If the glass is broken, sensors set off an alarm. Magnetic sensors are

often used on doors. One magnet is attached to the door, and a second is attached to the door frame. The two magnets are connected. If the door is opened, the magnetic connection is broken, sending a signal to the alarm system. **Infrared** sensors, made up of light we cannot see, can sense

Home security systems often have a keypad. Only the people living in the house know the code number to turn off the alarm.

the heat created by a human body. If a person enters an area where there are supposed to be no people, the alarm sounds.

BYTE-SIZED FACT

Smoke detectors save lives by alerting people to fires in their home or office. Some alarms contain a light source and a light-sensitive device called a photocell. Smoke scatters light from the source and reflects onto the photocell. This sets the alarm off. Other alarms use tiny, radioactive cells to electrically charge particles. These charged particles are called ions. The ions create a steady stream of electricity. Smoke particles attach to the ions and reduce the flow of electricity. This change sets off the alarm.

Machines at Work

"I need a faster computer."

Most workplaces use machines to help people do different tasks. Office machines may include anything from coffeemakers to calculators to robots that perform tasks people used to do. Machines in the workplace allow people to work more efficiently and more quickly. Companies rely on machines to make products quickly and cheaply.

New technology means the workplace is a constantly changing place. Workers must keep up with these changes by learning about new machines or computer programs. Some people argue that machines do too much work that could be done by people. Most people agree that machines help make the workplace more efficient by doing jobs that people cannot do or do not like to do.

How do photocopiers make copies?

Photocopiers copy words or images from a page or a book onto another piece of paper. To make a black-and-white copy, the page to be copied is placed on a piece of glass in the photocopier. The machine shines a bright light on the page. Light reflects off the white or light-colored parts of the page. The reflection of the page is transferred onto a round drum inside the copier. The drum contains a positive electric charge—positive charges result from an atom having fewer electrons or more protons. The light-colored areas lose this charge and become neutral.

Toner, which is the powdered ink in the photocopier, is applied to the drum. Toner carries a negative electrical charge—negative charges result from an atom having more electrons or fewer protons. The negative charge on the toner is attracted to the positive charge on the drum. The toner sticks to the dark areas on the drum, which have a positive charge. The dark toner on the drum is transferred to a clean piece of paper. The paper is then heated so that the ink becomes permanent, and the finished copy is ejected from the machine.

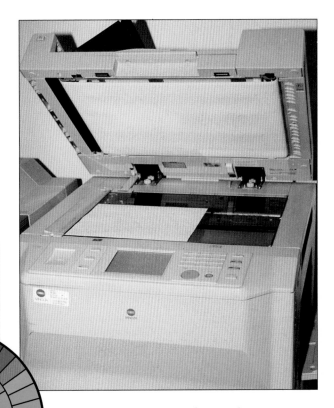

BYTE-SIZED FACT
Color photocopiers use only black plus three colors—cyan (blue), magenta (red), and yellow—to copy any color picture or photograph. Filters break down the original picture into the three different colors of light. By applying separate layers of black and of each color, the copier can duplicate any color on the original.

Photocopiers can make copies on different sizes of paper. Some copiers can enlarge or reduce the size of letters and images on a page to fit a larger or smaller piece of paper.

How do metal detectors work?

Security gates at airports and in other buildings use metal detectors to help prevent people from carrying guns, knives, and other weapons into a building or onto an airplane. An alarm sounds if a person walks through a security gate with something made of metal.

Simple transmission devices are made up of wire coils. Electricity is run through the coils, creating a magnetic field. When someone walks through the field with a piece of metal, the metal creates another magnetic field. This field reverses the flow of electricity in the first field. A message is sent to the detector indicating that metal is present. Then the machine's alarms sound.

Security guards check the person to see what might have set off the alarm. Guards can adjust the gate to go off only if someone is carrying a large amount of metal. Often, the coils in the gates are designed to sense any metal. Even a few coins in a pocket or the zipper on a jacket can set off an alarm.

Any metal in a person's pocket or on his or her clothing will activate the alarm.

BYTE-SIZED FACT

Handheld metal detectors can be used to find metal buried underground. These detectors create a small magnetic field. The detector is slowly moved over the ground. An alarm sounds when the magnetic field comes into contact with certain types of metal.

LINK TO
The Environment

Machines and Acid Rain

Acid rain is the term used to describe rain, snow, or other wet precipitation that has been contaminated by pollution. It is caused by high levels of certain chemicals in the air. These chemicals fall down to Earth with rain. Acid rain can harm plants and animals by damaging the places they live and the food they eat. It can also damage buildings.

Acid rain comes from many sources. The main causes are chemicals released into the air by machines. Factories that send harmful gases, such as sulfur dioxide and nitrogen oxide, into the air are the biggest sources of acid rain. Automobile engines are also some of the worst offenders. They give off harmful gases in their **emissions** when they burn gasoline.

Automobiles are required to have emission control devices. These devices lessen the amount of harmful chemicals that are released from automobile engines.

Emissions from factories and automobiles are made up of water vapor and other gases. Some of these gases harm the environment when they return to the ground as acid rain.

How does an elevator work?

Most buildings that are taller than three stories have elevators to move people and heavy objects to different floors. Elevators are boxes that move up and down on strong metal cables along elevator shafts, or well-like narrow spaces. Some elevators can travel to as many as 110 floors.

A pulley uses a wheel to support or guide a cable riding in a groove in its edge. Many elevators use a pulley system that is powered by an electric motor. Counterweights, heavy objects that move in the opposite direction of the elevator, help move the elevator box up and down more easily. The counterweights reduce the power that is needed to operate the elevator.

Passengers enter the elevator and press a button. An electric signal is sent from the button to the elevator control box. The control box tells the elevator which direction and floor the passenger has chosen. The pulley system then takes the elevator box to the correct floor.

The elevators on this tower at Niagara Falls are on the outside of the building. Passengers can enjoy the view while they ride up and down.

BYTE-SIZED FACT

Most elevators have safety features to protect passengers if the machine breaks down. If a cable breaks, these elevators have teeth that clamp onto the shaft so the box will not fall.

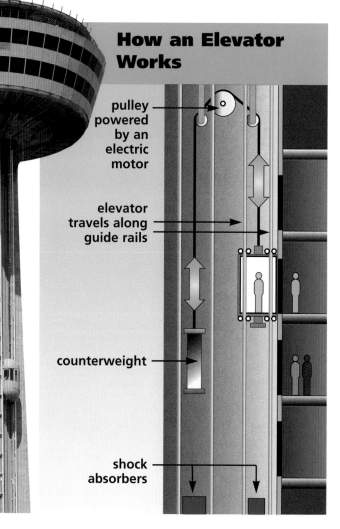

How an Elevator Works

pulley powered by an electric motor

elevator travels along guide rails

counterweight

shock absorbers

What do generators do?

Generators are machines that convert one form of energy into another kind of energy. They allow other machines to work. Electrical generators convert energy into electrical energy that can power lamps, household appliances, and other devices.

Power plants use large generators to produce electricity. Small, portable generators are useful during blackouts and in remote places where there is no access to power plants.

The first electrical generator was built by a scientist named Michael Faraday in 1831. Faraday discovered that when a coil of wire moves near a magnet, an electric current is created. When the magnet moves in one direction, current flows in one direction. When the magnet moves in the other direction, near the coil, the current in the wire flows in the opposite direction.

By moving the coil and the magnet back and forth, a continuous electric current is produced. Faraday made a device that had a rotating coil attached to a magnet. Other scientists have since improved this design.

BYTE-SIZED FACT

Fairs and exhibitions need a lot of electricity to power their lights and rides. Fairgrounds use large generators to make their own electricity. The generators sit on top of large trucks so that they can be driven from one town to another.

This electrical generator is small compared to the huge generators used in power plants.

How do vending machines work?

Vending machines allow us to buy drinks and candy from a machine instead of a person. Vending machines seem quite simple, but they must do many things at once. After you put money into the machine and make a choice, the drink or candy pops out of the machine. Each button on the vending machine is connected to a series of gears and levers. When you press a certain button, it will set these devices in motion, releasing your choice.

One of the most important devices in a vending machine is the coin sorter. It accepts and sorts coins. The sorter can tell which coin is which by the size and weight of the coin. Some machines even use sensors to check the metal content of the coins. **Counterfeit** coins are rejected by the machine. The sorter determines how much money was given and then spits out any change. While most vending machines accept coins, some also accept paper money. These machines scan, or look at, the bill to make sure it is real and to figure out how much it is worth.

Vending machines now offer more than treats. Some have meals including hamburgers and sandwiches.

BYTE-SIZED FACT

Some vending machines can keep food hot or cold. Cold vending machines work like refrigerators to keep their contents cool. Vending machines that sell hot drinks contain a water heater.

What are smart cards?

Many cards that people carry, including credit cards and bank cards, have magnetic strips on them. These strips contain a code number that allows access to the cardholder's account. Integrated circuit logic cards, also called smart cards, can do even more than cards with magnetic strips. Smart cards contain a **microchip**, a tiny piece of silicon onto which metal circuits are etched. It can hold more information than other cards. The microchip of a smart card may contain a cardholder's account information as well as a signature and a photograph. When the card is scanned, the information can be viewed on a computer screen.

Telephone cards are examples of smart cards. A telephone card allows a person to spend a certain amount of money on long-distance telephone calls. The card

Phone companies sell smart cards for use in payphones. This is great for people who never have the correct change to make a phone call.

keeps track of how much time is used. Department stores use smart cards instead of gift certificates. The staff member scans the card and reads how much money is left on the card and changes that total depending on the purchase. Smart cards are also used as identification cards or as security cards to allow certain people into locked buildings. One day we may all carry just one card that contains all the information we need to drive, use a bank machine, and enter buildings.

BYTE-SIZED FACT

The microchip on a smart card is made from metal and a tiny piece of **silicon**, an element that occurs in rocks and minerals. The microchip stores information electronically. It allows some information, such as how much money is left on a telephone card, to be altered. Other pieces of information, such as the cardholder's name, cannot be changed.

How is remote control used?

Many machines are not automatic—they need to be controlled by people. Remote control allows people to operate a machine from a distance. The operator of the machine uses a control box to change the movements of the machine. The control box sends messages to the machine either through long wires or radio waves.

Most of us use remote control every day in our own homes when we watch television. When a button is pressed on a television remote control, the information is sent to the television by infrared light signals. Infrared light cannot be seen by the human eye.

Television remote controls are especially useful for people who are ill or injured, making it hard for them to move around.

The television sensor picks up the infrared message, and the television makes the requested changes.

Remote control can also be used in situations that are dangerous to humans. It allows a person to control a machine without being in a dangerous area, such as near a bomb or deep under the sea.

Robots are used by police to pick up suspicious objects that may be bombs. The robots are operated by remote control so officers do not have to handle dangerous goods.

Robots in Industry

Robots are automated machines that can work and move like humans. They are often stronger than people and can do more detailed work than most machines or people.

Companies can save money and time by using robots. Robots can work around the clock. They do not need to take breaks or vacations. Some robots can do the same amount of work as several people.

Robots are often used to carry out tasks that are too difficult or too dangerous for people to carry out. Robots are used in many factories. Robots can also be built to do jobs that people find very boring, such as spray-painting thousands of car parts.

Most robots have the following parts: some moving parts, a drive system, a control

Several robots work at one time to weld metal pieces of a car together on an automobile assembly line.

center, and an end effector. The drive system gives the robot the power to move some of its parts. The control center is the "brain" of the robot. It tells the robot what to do and in what order. The control center may work by a remote control manipulated by a person, or it can be **programmed** like a small computer. The end effector is the part of the robot that completes the task, such as spray-painting car parts.

Unlike other machines, robots can respond to their surroundings. Electronic sensors allow them to "see" or "touch" the objects around them. This means that once robots have been programmed, people do not need to be directly involved in the work.

BYTE-SIZED FACT
Robots have been sent to the Moon and to Mars to collect soil samples and analyze them. The information is sent back to scientists on Earth.

How do computers help us work faster?

Computers have changed the way most people work. They can perform many tasks, such as addition and multiplication of numbers, faster than a person can. Computers can also help us create graphs and images much more quickly than we could draw them by hand.

The "brain" of a computer is its microprocessor. The microprocessor is the circuit that allows a computer to perform all of its tasks. In addition to working with numbers, the microprocessor can move information from one area in the computer's memory to another. It can also be programmed to make decisions depending on what the computer user has typed into the computer.

The hard disk is the part of a computer that stores all of its information. A hard disk works much the same way as a videocassette. It stores information as magnetic signals. Unlike a videocassette, a hard disk can store a huge amount of data.

BYTE-SIZED FACT

The first microprocessor, the Intel 4004, was invented in 1971. It could only add and subtract and was only able to work on four **bits**, or tiny pieces of information, at a time.

Computers can be used for work or play. Computers make both education and work faster and more enjoyable.

POINTS OF VIEW

Do Computers and Robots Take Jobs Away from People?

Computers and robots are used more and more in the workplace. These machines can be very helpful. They can work 24 hours a day. They can also work in dangerous environments. It is easier for some companies to use robots and computers than to use people to do the same jobs. Robots and computers often do tasks that could be done by people. In this way, these machines take jobs away from people. Many factories have replaced workers with robots.

Some people believe that we rely too much on these new machines. They believe that some of these machines cannot do certain jobs as well as people can. Another worry is that these new technologies will put many more people out of work.

Other people think we should use machines at work whenever we can. To them, machines make our lives easier and give us more free time. They believe that people who lose their jobs due to robots and computers can train in other fields and start new careers.

"It [robotics] is a great investment but it's hard to see a future for a lot of people."
Manager of an automobile plant that plans to use more robotics

"The personal touch is being lost."
Head of a workers' union commenting on use of computers in the workplace

"Technology will simply allow us to be more efficient and relieve staff from a lot of paper processing. It will allow us to devote more time to direct contact with the clients. At the same time, we can do it with fewer people."
Chairman of a company laying off workers because of increased use of computers

"Customers prefer to talk to a person rather than to a computer."
Manager of a retail store

Do you believe robots and computers take too many jobs away from people?

Machines for Transportation

"I'm taking the bus downtown."

Over the years, people have used many different machines for getting from one place to another. Bicycles are machines that provide a popular method of transportation. The invention of the steam engine meant that trains could transport people and goods quickly and farther away than horses and wagons could. Modern machines, such as automobiles and airplanes, have changed the way we view the world. These modern methods of transportation allow us to travel quickly across the country and around the globe. Most of these vehicles are powered by engines. These engines need fuel to work. As the fuels are burned, they pollute the environment. Engineers are trying to create new vehicles that are less damaging to the Earth.

What is the difference between a gasoline engine and a diesel engine?

Most vehicles use either gasoline or **diesel**, a type of light oil, as fuel. Gasoline engines are the most common. They are types of **internal combustion** engines. Fuel is burned in cylinders inside the engine. Cylinders are hollow metal tubes with circular walls.

There are two ways in which fuel is brought to a gas engine. In vehicles with carburetion systems, a device called a carburetor mixes air and gasoline. This mixture is sucked into the cylinders in the engine. Spark plugs ignite the mixture, causing small explosions. These explosions create hot gases that force down a piston, which is a cylinder-shaped plug that moves snugly up and down inside the cylinder. The movement of the pistons moves another device, called the crankshaft, which in turn moves the wheels of the vehicle. In fuel injected engines, which are found in most newer cars, the fuel is automatically put into each cylinder in the engine. Most gas engines use port fuel injection. This means the fuel is injected just above the intake valves of the cylinders.

Diesel engines work the same way as gas engines, except they do not need spark plugs. The fuel explosions are caused by heat and pressure created when diesel fuel is pressed into the cylinders. A diesel engine uses direct fuel injection.

This powerful gasoline engine has eight cylinders. Many automobile engines have four or six cylinders.

BYTE-SIZED FACT

The steam engine is an example of an external combustion engine. Internal combustion engines must use a pure liquid or gas fuel to run. Steam engines can use anything that burns as fuel, such as coal, wood, or even newspaper.

Non-Polluting Vehicles

One of the problems with most methods of transportation is that they release chemicals into the environment.

Vehicles other than bicycles release emissions into the air that can lead to acid rain and other types of pollution. Automobiles use **fossil fuels** such as oil and natural gas. These fossil fuels were created millions of years ago from the remains of dead plants and

Some companies have designed and built vehicles that are powered by fuel cells. These vehicles are not yet produced in large numbers.

animals. There are limited amounts of fossil fuels on Earth.

For many years, engineers have tried to create vehicles that do not pollute. In just a few years, many people may be driving electric vehicles, sometimes called EVs. EVs have engines that run on electricity instead of gasoline or diesel. Because they do not burn fuel, EVs do not release harmful emissions into the air. Some people do not believe that EVs are much better for the environment than automobiles that run on gasoline. This is because the generators that produce electricity to run EVs also pollute the environment.

Other cars are being designed to run on fuel cells that are powered by hydrogen, a gas. Hydrogen cars are considered to be the best for the environment. Instead of releasing dangerous emissions, hydrogen-powered cars only release water.

BYTE-SIZED FACT

Scientists have tried to use all types of substances, including sugar, to power cars. Sugar can be used to make a chemical called ethanol. When mixed with gasoline, ethanol creates fewer harmful emissions and uses less fossil fuel.

How was the first airplane made?

Many inventors hoped to be the first to create an engine-powered airplane. Gliders, which floated through the air without a motor, had been built, but no one could figure out how to make an airplane stay in the air. Scientists had determined how much power was needed to lift an object of a certain weight off the ground, but no one could keep an airplane in the air.

Two brothers named Orville and Wilbur Wright tried several times to build an airplane that would fly. In 1901 they built a wind tunnel, a tunnel for testing the effects of wind and air pressure on aircraft. They discovered that an airplane's wings had to be a certain length and width as compared to its body.

The Wrights built a glider that flew very well in a straight line, but crashed on turns. Then they built their first airplane called the Flyer. The engine was set at the pilot's right side, and it made two wooden propellers behind the wings move. The Wright brothers used a method of controlling the airplane called the wing warp system. Strings from the wings were attached to an apparatus

The Wright brothers' airplane was small and simple compared to modern planes. But in 1903, it was an amazing machine.

around the pilot's hips. By moving his hips, the pilot could pull up on one wing or the other to keep the plane balanced.

The Wrights decided to put a steering device called a **rudder** on the airplane. Rudders were already used to help steer boats. They built an engine for power and a propeller to move the airplane forward.

BYTE-SIZED FACT

The Wright brothers' first successful engine-powered airplane flight took place in 1903. The very first flight lasted only 12 seconds. Within a few tries, their airplane flew 852 feet (260 m) and stayed in the air 59 seconds.

What is a jet engine?

Airplanes have powerful engines to keep them in the air. Most large airplanes have jet engines. These engines, also called gas **turbine** engines, send hot air out the back of the airplane. This force moves the airplane forward. The jet engine burns jet fuel. The burning fuel heats up the air and makes it expand. This expanded, or pressurized, air then rushes out of the back of the engine. The air turns the turbine in the engine.

The front of a jet engine has an area to collect and compress, or squeeze, the incoming air. The air helps burn fuel. The burning fuel and air make a high-pressure gas, which is sent to the turbine. The movement of the gas makes the blades of the turbine spin, powering the airplane.

Very large jet planes use turbofan engines. These are the same as other gas turbine engines, except they have large fans at the front. These fans help bring even more air into the engine. A turboprop engine is similar to a turbofan engine, but has a propeller at the front of the engine instead of fans.

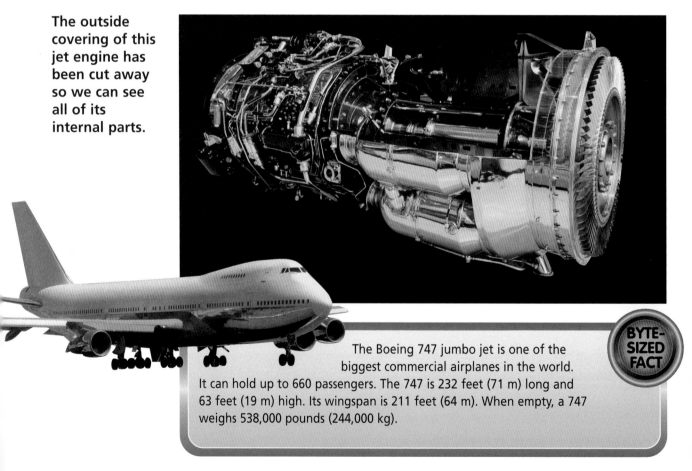

The outside covering of this jet engine has been cut away so we can see all of its internal parts.

The Boeing 747 jumbo jet is one of the biggest commercial airplanes in the world. It can hold up to 660 passengers. The 747 is 232 feet (71 m) long and 63 feet (19 m) high. Its wingspan is 211 feet (64 m). When empty, a 747 weighs 538,000 pounds (244,000 kg).

BYTE-SIZED FACT

Commercial Pilots

Commercial pilots fly planes for airline companies. These pilots transport passengers, goods, or mail across the country or around the world.

Most large passenger planes have two pilots: the captain and the copilot. Much of their work is done before the plane even leaves the ground.

Pilots check weather conditions, prepare a flight plan, and talk with the crew who will work with them on the plane. They then board the plane and check emergency equipment, flight instruments, radios, fuel supply, and other equipment.

In order to become a pilot, one must take special courses and spend many hours in flight training. Airplanes contain many types of machinery to help fly the plane and keep it safe. Different types of planes may contain different types of equipment.

Special computer systems, or autopilots, help the pilots work all the complicated machinery on a big jet plane. But pilots must know how all the systems work in case the systems fail during a flight.

Machines in Medicine

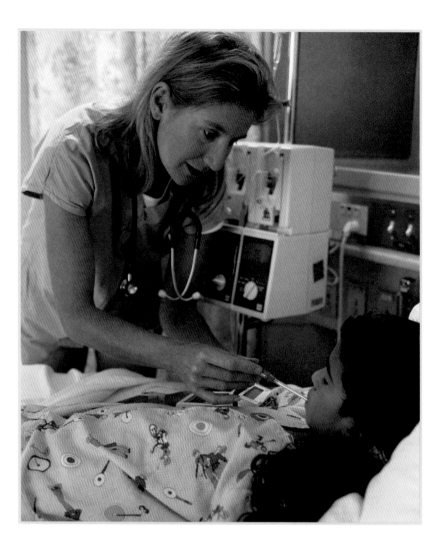

"We'll need to X-ray that leg."

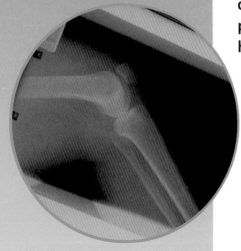

In the last century, medicine has gone through many changes. We can now help cure diseases and help save lives by using machines. Machines are used in all areas of medicine. They help doctors quickly diagnose, or determine, the cause of health problems. Machines are also used in surgery, and to help cure medical problems.

Simple machines, such as thermometers, have been used for many years. Newer machines, such as CAT scanners, are being used more and more to help find health problems before they can harm people. Health-care workers must know how to use modern medical equipment.

How do we take photographs of bones inside our bodies?

An X ray travels through a person's skin and muscle to take a photograph of the bones inside the body. Using these photographs, doctors can see if bones are broken without having to open the body.

An X ray is a type of invisible wave like a radio wave. X rays move through the body and are absorbed only by dense material such as bone. An X-ray machine has a tube that makes the rays and directs them onto the human body. The rays that pass through the body cause changes in the film that allow it to be developed into a visible image. The final image is called a **radiograph**. Bones show up as light or white areas on a radiograph. Other body parts appear black.

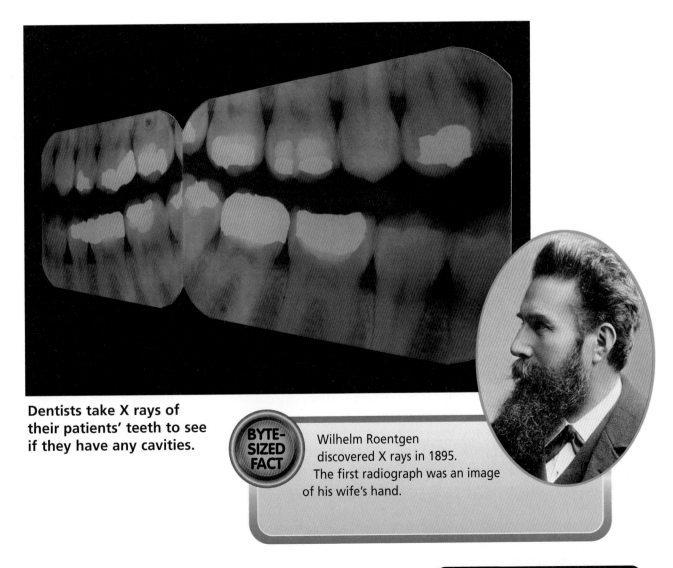

Dentists take X rays of their patients' teeth to see if they have any cavities.

BYTE-SIZED FACT

Wilhelm Roentgen discovered X rays in 1895. The first radiograph was an image of his wife's hand.

Can X rays Harm Our Health?

Most people have had some part of their body X-rayed at some time in their lives. Dentists regularly X-ray teeth and jaws to check for problems. X rays are a type of radiation, which is energy emitted through one body and absorbed into another. Too much radiation can be dangerous for people.

X rays expose people to small amounts of radiation, which is considered safe. People are exposed to small amounts of radiation from the environment every day. Sources of radiation include smoke detectors, television sets, some clocks, and building materials. There are even small amounts of radiation in some rocks and soil. This does not seem to harm our health. To protect people's health, X rays are only taken when absolutely necessary, and safety precautions are always used. The X rays are only shone on a person for a very short time. Parts of the body that are not being X-rayed are protected with a lead blanket.

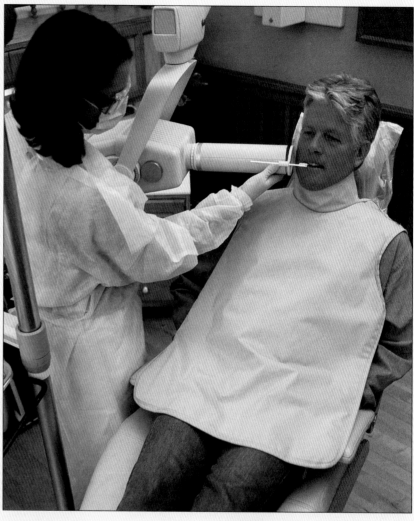

Special coverings or aprons protect patients when they are having dental X rays.

X-ray technicians work every day with machines that release radiation. These people wear protective clothing that blocks out radiation and stay at a distance from the X-ray machine.

BYTE-SIZED FACT

Radiation therapy uses powerful energy called radiation to kill cancer cells. Large, controlled amounts of this radiation can destroy cancer in the body or prevent the disease from spreading further.

How is blood pressure measured?

Blood pressure is the force with which blood moves through our arteries. Blood pressure is an important measure of a person's health. Blood pressure measurements are made up of two numbers. The higher number is the measurement of the systolic pressure. Systolic pressure is the maximum pressure as the heart pumps out blood. The lower number is of the diastolic pressure. This measures the lowest force used to move the blood through the arteries. This occurs when the blood is being pumped back into the heart and the heart is relaxed. Normal blood pressure is 120/80. If the numbers are too high, it shows that the heart is working too hard.

Blood pressure gauges consist of an inflatable cuff and a face that shows the pressure readings. Doctors and nurses measure blood pressure by placing the cuff around a person's upper arm. The cuff is filled with air to temporarily stop the flow of blood into the lower arm. The doctor then slowly releases the air while listening to the blood flow with a stethoscope placed on the inside of the elbow. As the air from the cuff is released, the doctor listens for the blood to start to flow. When this happens, the

Blood pressure usually rises as people get older. Their arteries become less elastic, and blood flow slows down through them.

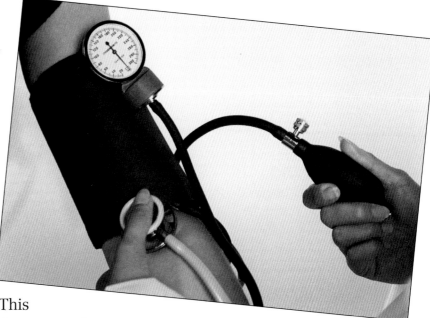

reading on the gauge is the systolic pressure. The doctor continues to listen until there is no longer any sound. At this point, the gauge reading shows the diastolic pressure.

BYTE-SIZED FACT

Stethoscopes are still used to listen to blood pressure. Electronic blood pressure gauges have microphones that pick up the pulsing noises of the blood. These are called Korothoff sounds. These devices are more accurate because they can detect sounds before a person can hear them through a stethoscope.

CAT Scanner

X-ray machines can take photographs of our bones, but they cannot take clear pictures of most other body parts. A Computerized Axial Tomographic, or CAT, scanner is a machine that can take photographs of the organs, such as the heart, liver, and kidneys, inside the body.

CAT scanners are used to get information about the brain, muscles, and organs. They can take images of these organs.

CAT scanners are very large machines. The patient lies on a table that moves through the center of the scanner. As the table moves, X-ray beams are sent through the patient's body from tubes that move in a circle around him or her. X-ray detectors on the machine collect the information. The information is digitized, or changed into computer signals. A computer turns the signals into a photo of a body organ.

CAT scans are painless. They can take from several minutes to one hour to complete.

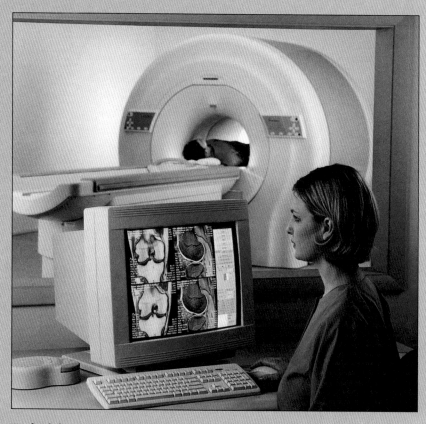

Technicians use a computer to record images of a patient's body. These images help doctors determine how to treat the patient.

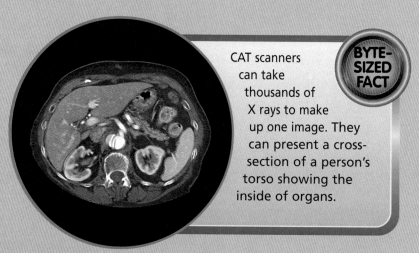

CAT scanners can take thousands of X rays to make up one image. They can present a cross-section of a person's torso showing the inside of organs.

BYTE-SIZED FACT

How do digital thermometers measure our body temperature?

Thermometers were once made from glass with a scale marked on it to show the temperature values. Thermometers contained a liquid called mercury. Mercury is an element that is very dangerous to humans if it is swallowed. To measure a person's temperature, these thermometers had to be placed under the tongue for three minutes. As the temperature became higher, the mercury would rise in the glass. A person could tell the temperature by reading how high up the glass the mercury rose.

Although mercury thermometers are still used today, digital thermometers work much faster and are safer. The digital thermometer is made up of several parts. It gets its power from a tiny battery, much like the ones used in digital watches.

The tip of the thermometer contains a small device that is sensitive to heat. It reads the temperature as electrical signals and sends the information to a sensor. The sensor reads these signals and translates them into a series of temperature numbers, or readings. It would take a few minutes for the thermometer to reach the exact temperature reading. Electronic thermometers work faster by calculating what the final temperature will be from

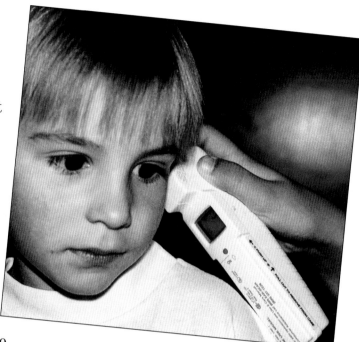

The speed of digital thermometers is useful when treating young children. Children need to sit still for only seconds.

the early temperatures, which slowly rise toward the actual number. The microprocessor inside the thermometer takes all the temperature numbers, or readings, and predicts what the final temperature will be. In this way, the thermometer can accurately read a person's temperature in under 30 seconds. The temperature will be the same as, or very close to, the actual temperature. The temperature is displayed as a number on the side of the thermometer.

What is an ECG?

An ECG, or electrocardiogram, is a machine that records a person's heartbeat. Devices called **electrodes**, which conduct electric current, are usually attached to the patient's body using a clear jelly. Before the heart beats, it makes a small electrical current that makes the heart muscles contract. The electrodes measure these currents as wave patterns. They send the information to the electrocardiograph. The machine prints out an image of the heart changes. A normal ECG looks like a line of waves all the same height. Abnormal heartbeats have waves that are closer or farther apart than others, or go lower or higher. An ECG showing an irregular heartbeat can help doctors tell whether a patient has heart problems. Different heart diseases have different types of ECGs.

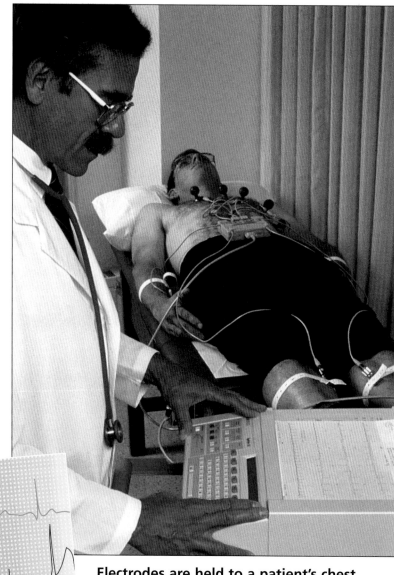

The top of this readout shows signals from a healthy man's heart. The bottom shows those from the heart of a 60-year-old man with chest pains.

Electrodes are held to a patient's chest and legs with tape. The doctor analyzes the signals on an electrocardiograph.

Ultrasound Technician

Ultrasound scanners give off ultrasonic waves, which are sounds that people cannot hear. These waves bounce off different parts inside the body and send back an echo. Ultrasound machines then change the echoes into pictures that can be examined by a doctor or technician.

Ultrasound machines are used to create images, called **sonograms**, of the shape and movement of blood, internal organs, and other body tissues. Ultrasound is often used to check the health of an unborn baby, to check for abnormal heart movements, and to check for any unusual growths in the body. Ultrasound technologists work in hospitals or in medical clinics. They are trained to use ultrasound equipment to gain information about patients. They then report their findings to doctors. They also review the medical information about a patient and help teach patients about good health.

Unlike some other medical procedures, such as X rays, ultrasounds are considered completely safe. Because of this, the use of ultrasound is becoming more popular, and there is a demand for more ultrasound technicians.

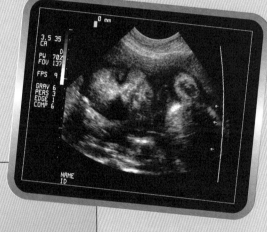

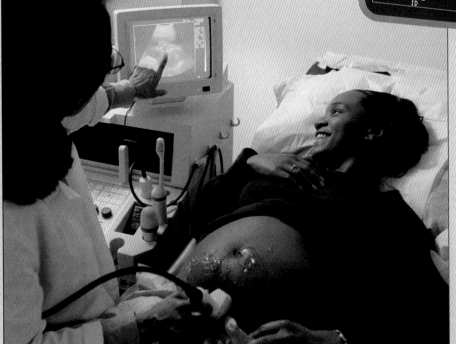

Ultrasound is popular because it can show detailed information without having to open the body. Ultrasound poses no threat to the mother or the baby.

Science Survey

You probably use many of the machines mentioned in this book. Most of us have refrigerators and washing machines in our homes. We use computers either at home, school, or work. We may also use calculators, televisions, telephones, and radios in our daily lives.

What Are Your Answers?

1. Do you have a telephone at home? How many phones do you have?
2. Do you own a radio? How many radios does your family have?
3. Is there a television at home? How many?
4. Do you own at least one videocassette recorder?
5. Do you have a computer at home? If not, do you use a computer at school or anywhere else?

Survey Results

In the United States, 93.9 percent of all homes have a telephone. Ninety-nine percent of all homes have at least one radio. On average, every household has 5.6 radios. Most homes, 98.3 percent, have at least one television. On average, each home has 2.3 televisions. Eighty-one percent of households have a videocassette recorder. Of children aged 3 to 17, only 32 percent have computers at home. Nearly 60 percent of children use a computer at home, at school, or elsewhere.

Here is your challenge:

Try to be aware of all the machines you use every day. On a piece of paper, make two columns. In the first column, write down all of the machines that you think you use often, such as a microwave oven, a computer, or the telephone.

For one week, put a check mark in the second column each time you use a particular machine. Make sure you add any new machines that were not on your list.

At the end of the week, add up the check marks to see which machines you use the most. Try to imagine what your life would be like without these machines. Circle the machines that are most important to you.

Fast Facts

1. Archimedes, a mathematician in ancient Greece, supposedly invented a machine that can raise water from deep under the ground. The Archimedean screw is still used today.

2. The first electronic calculator was invented in 1963 and was as large as a cash register. Today calculators can fit into a wristwatch.

3. *Sputnik I*, the first satellite, was sent into orbit around the Earth in 1957. Satellites are now used for space research, weather prediction, and communication.

4. Bomb disposal robots are used to dismantle bombs before they blow up.

5. In 1976 the world's fastest commercial airplane, the Concorde, began carrying passengers. The Concorde flies at about 1,500 miles per hour (2,410 kph).

6. The wheel is one of the simplest but most important machines in the world. The first wheel was invented around 3500 B.C.

7. Computers contain tiny silicon chips. These chips have electrical circuits that can store enormous amounts of information.

8. Fax machines change words and images into electric signals that can be sent over telephone lines. When the signals reach another fax machine, they are converted back to words and images.

9. Radar (Radio Detection And Ranging) was developed over a period of 40 years. It helped airplanes and ships see other objects in the dark during World War II.

10. The fastest trains in the world are powered by electricity.

11. Many modern clocks and watches contain the mineral quartz. An electric current makes the quartz crystals vibrate at a constant rate.

12. The film in Polaroid cameras develops as soon as the picture is taken. The film contains all of the chemicals needed to develop the photograph.

13. Long ago, water was used to tell time. Water was placed in a large container with a small hole in the bottom. People could tell how much time had passed by the level of water left in the container.

14. The first personal computers had 256 bytes of memory. Many computers today have 16 million bytes of memory.

15. The best temperature for the inside of a refrigerator is 35 to 38°F (2 to 3°C).

16. Videocassette recorders can record television programs at three different speeds. The quality of the sounds and images decreases as the recording speed decreases.

17. Solar cars use power from the Sun to run. These cars do not pollute the environment.

18. The first practical safety elevator was invented by an American named Elisha Otis more than 100 years ago.

19. A Magnetic Resonance Imaging (MRI) machine uses magnets to make the human body produce radio waves. A computer changes these waves into images of the inside of the body so that doctors can see problems that might affect the patient's health.

20. In the 1800s steam was used to power engines in trains. Steam engines are a type of external combustion engine.

You can learn more about the way machines work by doing the following activities. Experiment by building simple machines on your own.

Make a Sundial

What you need:
- a long, thin stick or a ruler
- a large piece of light-colored paper
- a pencil

Activity

Using the sharp tip of a pencil, make a small hole in the middle of the piece of paper. Be careful not to stick your finger.

In the morning, place the paper on a flat piece of ground in a sunny area outside. Take the ruler or stick, and place it through the hole in the paper into the ground. Make sure that the stick is placed far enough into the ground that it and the paper will not move.

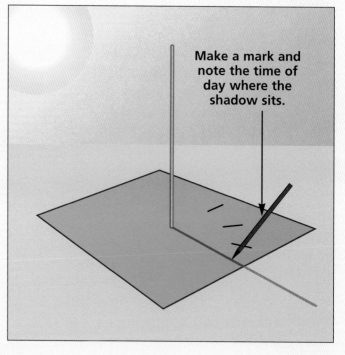

Make a mark and note the time of day where the shadow sits.

The Sun will shine down and create a shadow from the stick on the paper. Every hour, mark where the shadow is on the piece of paper. Also write down the time of day.

At the end of the day, you will have your own clock. If you look at it the next day, you should be able to see what time it is just by looking at the stick's shadow on the paper.

Make a Pinhole Camera

What you need:

- a large aluminum can, such as a coffee can, open at one end
- a piece of black construction paper
- tape
- a hammer
- a small nail
- a piece of waxed paper
- scissors
- a rubber band

Activity

Have an adult help you punch a small hole in the center of the can's closed end using the hammer and nail.

Cover the open end of the can with waxed paper, using the rubber band to hold the waxed paper in place.

Wrap the construction paper around the outside of the can. About 10 inches (25 cm) of construction paper should extend past the end of the can covered with waxed paper. Tape the construction paper securely to the can.

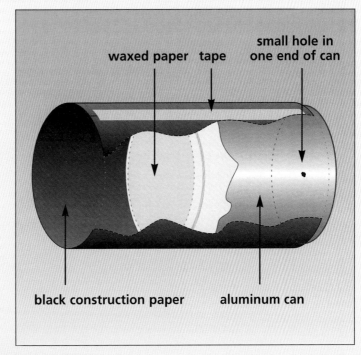

waxed paper   tape   small hole in one end of can

black construction paper   aluminum can

In a dark room, point the hole in the can toward a window. Hold the other end of the can up to your eyes. Look through the black paper tunnel to the waxed paper.

You should be able to see an image on the waxed paper. Can you figure out why the image is upside down?

Research on Your Own

There are many places to learn about the science of machines. Your local library and the Internet are good places to start. They have excellent information for you. Here are some awesome resources to try.

Great Books

Hewitt, Sally. *Machines We Use.* Children's Press, 1998.

Machines (Picturepedia). Edited by Hilary Hockman. Toronto: Stoddart, 1995.

Oxlade, Chris. *Learn about Machines.* London: Lorenz Books, 1998.

Parker, Steve. *Computers.* Austin, TX: Raintree Steck-Vaughn, 1997.

Parker, Steve. *Medical Advances.* Austin, TX: Raintree Steck-Vaughn, 1998.

Great Websites

How Stuff Works
http://www.howstuffworks.com

How Things Work
http://howthingswork.virginia.edu

The Science Explorer
http://www.exploratorium.edu/science_explorer/

Glossary

bit: The smallest unit of information stored by a computer

CAT scanner: A machine used to take images of the inside of the body

counterfeit: Imitation or fake

develop: When chemicals are added to photographic film to create final photographs

diagnose: To determine the cause of illness after performing and evaluating medical tests

diesel: A type of light oil used as fuel in some engines

electrode: A device that conducts an electric current

emissions: The gases that are released from a vehicle's exhaust pipes

fossil fuels: Fuels, such as coal, oil, and natural gas, that were created millions of years ago from the remains of plants and animals

frequency: The number of times an electric wave vibrates each second

friction: The action or resistance of two objects moving against one another

infrared: Long light waves that are not visible to the human eye

internal combustion: When fuel burns inside an engine

microbe: A living organism too small to see without a microscope

microchip: Tiny machines, smaller than a fingernail, that make computers and other electronic devices work

program: To create a set of instructions that a computer must follow

radiation: High-energy particles or rays that can cause damage to living tissue

radiograph: The image created by an X-ray machine

rudder: A device attached to the back of a boat or an airplane used to steer it

sensor: A device that responds to light, heat, or motion

silicon: A nonmetallic element from which microchips are made

sonogram: The image of the inside of a person's body created by ultrasound equipment

turbine: A machine that has a rotor with blades. Turbines can be powered by steam, water, or air.

vaporize: When a liquid turns to a gas

Index

acid rain 17, 28
airplane 4, 5, 16, 26, 29, 30, 31,
   42, 47

bit 24, 47

calculator 14, 40, 42
cameras 12, 43, 45
CAT scan 5, 32, 36
clocks 4, 11, 43, 44
computer 5, 14, 23, 24, 25, 36,
   40, 41, 42, 43, 46, 47

ECG 38
electrodes 38, 47
elevator 18, 43
emissions 17, 28, 47
engines 5, 17, 26, 27, 28, 29,
   30, 43, 47
external combustion 27, 43

fax 42
friction 7, 47

generator 19, 28

internal combustion 27, 47

metal detector 16
microchip 21, 47
microwave ovens 7, 41

photocopier 15
pilot 5, 29, 31

quartz 43

radar 43
radiation 7, 34, 47
radiograph 33, 47
refrigerators 5, 8, 20, 40, 43
remote control 4, 22, 23
robot 14, 23, 25, 42
rudder 29, 47

satellite 42
security systems 13
sensor 13, 20, 22, 23, 37, 47
smart cards 21
sonogram 39, 47

thermometer 32, 37
turbine 30, 47

ultrasound technologist 39

vending machines 20
videocassette recorders 9, 24, 41, 43

washing machine 10, 40
watch 11, 37, 42, 43
wheel 4, 11, 18, 27, 42

X ray 5, 32, 33, 34, 36, 39